Time to Sleep

Jill McDougall

Illustrated by James Hart

Zzzzz-z

Contents

CU00801141

How Do You Sleep?

How do you sleep at bedtime?

Do you sleep on one leg?

Some animals do.

Do you sleep in a tree?

Some animals do!

Animals sleep in all sorts of ways.

Upside Down

Bats sleep upside down.

They hang from branches by their feet.

They can fly away if they are in danger.

Zzzzzzzzz

Could you sleep
upside down?

Standing Up

Horses can sleep standing up.

They do not fall over.

They can run away if they are scared.

Could you sleep standing up?

One Eye Open

Dolphins sleep with one eye open.
They can see where they are going
while they are sleeping.
They can look out for danger.

Could you sleep with one eye open?

9

On One Leg

Ducks sleep on one leg.
They tuck the other leg under their feathers.
One duck looks out for danger.

Zzzzzzzzz

Could you sleep on one leg?

In a Tree

Koalas sleep in trees.

They sleep for most of the day.

They feel safe when they are up high.

Zzzzzzzz

Could you sleep
in a tree?

13

Anywhere!

Cats like to sleep a lot.
They sleep in all sorts of ways.
They sleep anywhere!

Zzzzzzzzzz

Picture Index